THIS BOOK BELONGS TO:

CONTACT INFORMATION	
NAME:	
ADDRESS:	
PHONE:	

START / END DATES

___ / ___ / ___   TO   ___ / ___ / ___

Dedication

This Off Roading Log Book is dedicated to all the extreme sport enthusiasts out there who want to record all their off roading adventures and document their findings in the process.

You are my inspiration for producing books and I'm honored to be a part of keeping all of your off roading notes and records organized.

This journal notebook will help you record the details of your off roading adventures.

Thoughtfully put together with these sections to record: Date, Location, Passes Needed, Group/ Organization, Trail Conditions, Checklist, Observations, & Conclusions.

How to Use this Book

The purpose of this book is to keep all of your Off Roading notes all in one place. It will help keep you organized.

This Off Roading Log will allow you to accurately document every detail about your ATV & UTV adventures.

Here are examples of the prompts for you to fill in and write about your experience in this book:

1. Date - Write the date.

2. Location - Record the location.

3. Pass Needed - Log any pass that you need.

4. Group or Organization - For writing down the land owner, group or organization.

5. Checklist - Checklist includes Tire Pressure & Spares, Belts & Hoses, Bolts & Lug Nuts, Winch & Batteries, Assorted Tools, All Fluids, Brake Pads & Shoes, Shocks & Mounts, All Spare Gas Tanks, & Fording Depths & Angles.

6. Trail Conditions - Write what the conditions of the trails are.

7. Observations - Record anything you see that you might want to write down, or ideas.

8. Conclusions - Do you recommend overall, was it well managed, was it challenging, trail's reputation, overall score 1-10.

Off Roading Log

DATE	LOCATION
PASS NEEDED	
DAILY MEMBERSHIP PARK PERMIT	LAND OWNER ORGANIZATION NATIONAL PARK

GROUP OR ORGANIZATION

CHECKLIST

o TIRE PRESSURES & SPARE(S)	o ALL FLUIDS
o BELTS & HOSES	o BRAKE PADS & SHOES
o ALL BOLTS & LUG NUTS	o SHOCKS & MOUNTS
o WINCH & BATTERIES	o ALL SPARE GAS TANKS
o ASSORTED TOOLS	o FORDING DEPTHS & ANGLES

TRAIL CONDITIONS

OBSERVATIONS

CONCLUSIONS

YES	NO	SHADE ONE	TRAIL REPUTATION	SCORE
o	o	RECOMMEND OVERALL?		
o	o	WELL MANAGED?		
o	o	CHALLENGING?	1 TO 10	1 TO 10

Off Roading Log

DATE	LOCATION
PASS NEEDED	
DAILY MEMBERSHIP PARK PERMIT	LAND OWNER ORGANIZATION NATIONAL PARK

GROUP OR ORGANIZATION

CHECKLIST

○ TIRE PRESSURES & SPARE(S)	○ ALL FLUIDS
○ BELTS & HOSES	○ BRAKE PADS & SHOES
○ ALL BOLTS & LUG NUTS	○ SHOCKS & MOUNTS
○ WINCH & BATTERIES	○ ALL SPARE GAS TANKS
○ ASSORTED TOOLS	○ FORDING DEPTHS & ANGLES

TRAIL CONDITIONS

OBSERVATIONS

CONCLUSIONS

YES	NO	SHADE ONE	TRAIL REPUTATION	SCORE
○	○	RECOMMEND OVERALL?		
○	○	WELL MANAGED?		
○	○	CHALLENGING?	1 TO 10	1 TO 10

Off Roading Log

DATE	LOCATION
PASS NEEDED	
DAILY MEMBERSHIP PARK PERMIT	LAND OWNER ORGANIZATION NATIONAL PARK

GROUP OR ORGANIZATION

CHECKLIST	
o TIRE PRESSURES & SPARE(S)	o ALL FLUIDS
o BELTS & HOSES	o BRAKE PADS & SHOES
o ALL BOLTS & LUG NUTS	o SHOCKS & MOUNTS
o WINCH & BATTERIES	o ALL SPARE GAS TANKS
o ASSORTED TOOLS	o FORDING DEPTHS & ANGLES

TRAIL CONDITIONS

OBSERVATIONS

CONCLUSIONS				
YES	NO	SHADE ONE	TRAIL REPUTATION	SCORE
o	o	RECOMMEND OVERALL?		
o	o	WELL MANAGED?		
o	o	CHALLENGING?	1 TO 10	1 TO 10

Off Roading Log

DATE	LOCATION
PASS NEEDED	
DAILY MEMBERSHIP PARK PERMIT	LAND OWNER ORGANIZATION NATIONAL PARK

GROUP OR ORGANIZATION

CHECKLIST

o TIRE PRESSURES & SPARE(S)	o ALL FLUIDS
o BELTS & HOSES	o BRAKE PADS & SHOES
o ALL BOLTS & LUG NUTS	o SHOCKS & MOUNTS
o WINCH & BATTERIES	o ALL SPARE GAS TANKS
o ASSORTED TOOLS	o FORDING DEPTHS & ANGLES

TRAIL CONDITIONS

OBSERVATIONS

CONCLUSIONS

YES	NO	SHADE ONE	TRAIL REPUTATION	SCORE
o	o	RECOMMEND OVERALL?		
o	o	WELL MANAGED?		
o	o	CHALLENGING?	1 TO 10	1 TO 10

Off Roading Log

DATE	LOCATION
PASS NEEDED	
DAILY MEMBERSHIP PARK PERMIT	LAND OWNER ORGANIZATION NATIONAL PARK

GROUP OR ORGANIZATION

CHECKLIST	
○ TIRE PRESSURES & SPARE(S)	○ ALL FLUIDS
○ BELTS & HOSES	○ BRAKE PADS & SHOES
○ ALL BOLTS & LUG NUTS	○ SHOCKS & MOUNTS
○ WINCH & BATTERIES	○ ALL SPARE GAS TANKS
○ ASSORTED TOOLS	○ FORDING DEPTHS & ANGLES

TRAIL CONDITIONS

OBSERVATIONS

CONCLUSIONS				
YES	NO	SHADE ONE	TRAIL REPUTATION	SCORE
○	○	RECOMMEND OVERALL?		
○	○	WELL MANAGED?		
○	○	CHALLENGING?	1 TO 10	1 TO 10

Off Roading Log

DATE	LOCATION
PASS NEEDED	
DAILY MEMBERSHIP PARK PERMIT	LAND OWNER ORGANIZATION NATIONAL PARK

GROUP OR ORGANIZATION

CHECKLIST

○ TIRE PRESSURES & SPARE(S)	○ ALL FLUIDS
○ BELTS & HOSES	○ BRAKE PADS & SHOES
○ ALL BOLTS & LUG NUTS	○ SHOCKS & MOUNTS
○ WINCH & BATTERIES	○ ALL SPARE GAS TANKS
○ ASSORTED TOOLS	○ FORDING DEPTHS & ANGLES

TRAIL CONDITIONS

OBSERVATIONS

CONCLUSIONS

YES	NO	SHADE ONE	TRAIL REPUTATION	SCORE
○	○	RECOMMEND OVERALL?		
○	○	WELL MANAGED?		
○	○	CHALLENGING?	1 TO 10	1 TO 10

Off Roading Log

DATE	LOCATION
PASS NEEDED	
DAILY MEMBERSHIP PARK PERMIT	LAND OWNER ORGANIZATION NATIONAL PARK

GROUP OR ORGANIZATION

CHECKLIST

○ TIRE PRESSURES & SPARE(S)	○ ALL FLUIDS
○ BELTS & HOSES	○ BRAKE PADS & SHOES
○ ALL BOLTS & LUG NUTS	○ SHOCKS & MOUNTS
○ WINCH & BATTERIES	○ ALL SPARE GAS TANKS
○ ASSORTED TOOLS	○ FORDING DEPTHS & ANGLES

TRAIL CONDITIONS

OBSERVATIONS

CONCLUSIONS

YES	NO	SHADE ONE	TRAIL REPUTATION	SCORE
○	○	RECOMMEND OVERALL?		
○	○	WELL MANAGED?		
○	○	CHALLENGING?	1 TO 10	1 TO 10

Off Roading Log

DATE	LOCATION
PASS NEEDED	
DAILY MEMBERSHIP PARK PERMIT	LAND OWNER ORGANIZATION NATIONAL PARK

GROUP OR ORGANIZATION

CHECKLIST

○ TIRE PRESSURES & SPARE(S)	○ ALL FLUIDS
○ BELTS & HOSES	○ BRAKE PADS & SHOES
○ ALL BOLTS & LUG NUTS	○ SHOCKS & MOUNTS
○ WINCH & BATTERIES	○ ALL SPARE GAS TANKS
○ ASSORTED TOOLS	○ FORDING DEPTHS & ANGLES

TRAIL CONDITIONS

OBSERVATIONS

CONCLUSIONS

YES	NO	SHADE ONE	TRAIL REPUTATION	SCORE
○	○	RECOMMEND OVERALL?		
○	○	WELL MANAGED?		
○	○	CHALLENGING?	1 TO 10	1 TO 10

Off Roading Log

DATE	LOCATION
PASS NEEDED	
DAILY MEMBERSHIP PARK PERMIT	LAND OWNER ORGANIZATION NATIONAL PARK

GROUP OR ORGANIZATION

CHECKLIST

○ TIRE PRESSURES & SPARE(S)	○ ALL FLUIDS
○ BELTS & HOSES	○ BRAKE PADS & SHOES
○ ALL BOLTS & LUG NUTS	○ SHOCKS & MOUNTS
○ WINCH & BATTERIES	○ ALL SPARE GAS TANKS
○ ASSORTED TOOLS	○ FORDING DEPTHS & ANGLES

TRAIL CONDITIONS

OBSERVATIONS

CONCLUSIONS

YES	NO	SHADE ONE	TRAIL REPUTATION	SCORE
○	○	RECOMMEND OVERALL?		
○	○	WELL MANAGED?		
○	○	CHALLENGING?	1 TO 10	1 TO 10

Off Roading Log

DATE	LOCATION
PASS NEEDED	
DAILY MEMBERSHIP PARK PERMIT	LAND OWNER ORGANIZATION NATIONAL PARK

GROUP OR ORGANIZATION

CHECKLIST	
○ TIRE PRESSURES & SPARE(S)	○ ALL FLUIDS
○ BELTS & HOSES	○ BRAKE PADS & SHOES
○ ALL BOLTS & LUG NUTS	○ SHOCKS & MOUNTS
○ WINCH & BATTERIES	○ ALL SPARE GAS TANKS
○ ASSORTED TOOLS	○ FORDING DEPTHS & ANGLES

TRAIL CONDITIONS

OBSERVATIONS

CONCLUSIONS			
YES	NO	SHADE ONE	TRAIL REPUTATION	SCORE
○	○	RECOMMEND OVERALL?		
○	○	WELL MANAGED?		
○	○	CHALLENGING?	1 TO 10	1 TO 10

Off Roading Log

DATE	LOCATION
PASS NEEDED	
DAILY MEMBERSHIP PARK PERMIT	LAND OWNER ORGANIZATION NATIONAL PARK

GROUP OR ORGANIZATION

CHECKLIST	
○ TIRE PRESSURES & SPARE(S)	○ ALL FLUIDS
○ BELTS & HOSES	○ BRAKE PADS & SHOES
○ ALL BOLTS & LUG NUTS	○ SHOCKS & MOUNTS
○ WINCH & BATTERIES	○ ALL SPARE GAS TANKS
○ ASSORTED TOOLS	○ FORDING DEPTHS & ANGLES

TRAIL CONDITIONS

OBSERVATIONS

CONCLUSIONS				
YES	NO	SHADE ONE	TRAIL REPUTATION	SCORE
○	○	RECOMMEND OVERALL?		
○	○	WELL MANAGED?		
○	○	CHALLENGING?	1 TO 10	1 TO 10

Off Roading Log

DATE	LOCATION
PASS NEEDED	
DAILY MEMBERSHIP PARK PERMIT	LAND OWNER ORGANIZATION NATIONAL PARK

GROUP OR ORGANIZATION	

CHECKLIST	
○ TIRE PRESSURES & SPARE(S)	○ ALL FLUIDS
○ BELTS & HOSES	○ BRAKE PADS & SHOES
○ ALL BOLTS & LUG NUTS	○ SHOCKS & MOUNTS
○ WINCH & BATTERIES	○ ALL SPARE GAS TANKS
○ ASSORTED TOOLS	○ FORDING DEPTHS & ANGLES

TRAIL CONDITIONS	

OBSERVATIONS	

CONCLUSIONS					
YES	NO	SHADE ONE	TRAIL REPUTATION	SCORE
○	○	RECOMMEND OVERALL?		
○	○	WELL MANAGED?		
○	○	CHALLENGING?	1 TO 10	1 TO 10

Off Roading Log

DATE	LOCATION
PASS NEEDED	
DAILY MEMBERSHIP PARK PERMIT	LAND OWNER ORGANIZATION NATIONAL PARK

GROUP OR ORGANIZATION

CHECKLIST

o TIRE PRESSURES & SPARE(S)	o ALL FLUIDS
o BELTS & HOSES	o BRAKE PADS & SHOES
o ALL BOLTS & LUG NUTS	o SHOCKS & MOUNTS
o WINCH & BATTERIES	o ALL SPARE GAS TANKS
o ASSORTED TOOLS	o FORDING DEPTHS & ANGLES

TRAIL CONDITIONS

OBSERVATIONS

CONCLUSIONS

YES	NO	SHADE ONE	TRAIL REPUTATION	SCORE
o	o	RECOMMEND OVERALL?		
o	o	WELL MANAGED?		
o	o	CHALLENGING?	1 TO 10	1 TO 10

Off Roading Log

DATE	LOCATION
PASS NEEDED	
DAILY MEMBERSHIP PARK PERMIT	LAND OWNER ORGANIZATION NATIONAL PARK

GROUP OR ORGANIZATION

CHECKLIST	
o TIRE PRESSURES & SPARE(S)	o ALL FLUIDS
o BELTS & HOSES	o BRAKE PADS & SHOES
o ALL BOLTS & LUG NUTS	o SHOCKS & MOUNTS
o WINCH & BATTERIES	o ALL SPARE GAS TANKS
o ASSORTED TOOLS	o FORDING DEPTHS & ANGLES

TRAIL CONDITIONS

OBSERVATIONS

CONCLUSIONS				
YES	NO	SHADE ONE	TRAIL REPUTATION	SCORE
o	o	RECOMMEND OVERALL?		
o	o	WELL MANAGED?		
o	o	CHALLENGING?	1 TO 10	1 TO 10

Off Roading Log

DATE	LOCATION

PASS NEEDED	
DAILY MEMBERSHIP PARK PERMIT	LAND OWNER ORGANIZATION NATIONAL PARK

GROUP OR ORGANIZATION	

CHECKLIST	
o TIRE PRESSURES & SPARE(S)	o ALL FLUIDS
o BELTS & HOSES	o BRAKE PADS & SHOES
o ALL BOLTS & LUG NUTS	o SHOCKS & MOUNTS
o WINCH & BATTERIES	o ALL SPARE GAS TANKS
o ASSORTED TOOLS	o FORDING DEPTHS & ANGLES

TRAIL CONDITIONS	

OBSERVATIONS	

CONCLUSIONS				
YES	NO	SHADE ONE	TRAIL REPUTATION	SCORE
○	○	RECOMMEND OVERALL?		
○	○	WELL MANAGED?		
○	○	CHALLENGING?	1 TO 10	1 TO 10

Off Roading Log

DATE	LOCATION
PASS NEEDED	
DAILY MEMBERSHIP PARK PERMIT	LAND OWNER ORGANIZATION NATIONAL PARK

GROUP OR ORGANIZATION

CHECKLIST	
o TIRE PRESSURES & SPARE(S)	o ALL FLUIDS
o BELTS & HOSES	o BRAKE PADS & SHOES
o ALL BOLTS & LUG NUTS	o SHOCKS & MOUNTS
o WINCH & BATTERIES	o ALL SPARE GAS TANKS
o ASSORTED TOOLS	o FORDING DEPTHS & ANGLES

TRAIL CONDITIONS

OBSERVATIONS

CONCLUSIONS				
YES	NO	SHADE ONE	TRAIL REPUTATION	SCORE
o	o	RECOMMEND OVERALL?		
o	o	WELL MANAGED?		
o	o	CHALLENGING?	1 TO 10	1 TO 10

Off Roading Log

DATE	LOCATION

PASS NEEDED	
DAILY MEMBERSHIP PARK PERMIT	LAND OWNER ORGANIZATION NATIONAL PARK

GROUP OR ORGANIZATION

CHECKLIST

○ TIRE PRESSURES & SPARE(S)	○ ALL FLUIDS
○ BELTS & HOSES	○ BRAKE PADS & SHOES
○ ALL BOLTS & LUG NUTS	○ SHOCKS & MOUNTS
○ WINCH & BATTERIES	○ ALL SPARE GAS TANKS
○ ASSORTED TOOLS	○ FORDING DEPTHS & ANGLES

TRAIL CONDITIONS

OBSERVATIONS

CONCLUSIONS

YES	NO	SHADE ONE	TRAIL REPUTATION	SCORE
○	○	RECOMMEND OVERALL?		
○	○	WELL MANAGED?		
○	○	CHALLENGING?	1 TO 10	1 TO 10

Off Roading Log

DATE	LOCATION
PASS NEEDED	
DAILY MEMBERSHIP PARK PERMIT	LAND OWNER ORGANIZATION NATIONAL PARK

GROUP OR ORGANIZATION

CHECKLIST	
○ TIRE PRESSURES & SPARE(S)	○ ALL FLUIDS
○ BELTS & HOSES	○ BRAKE PADS & SHOES
○ ALL BOLTS & LUG NUTS	○ SHOCKS & MOUNTS
○ WINCH & BATTERIES	○ ALL SPARE GAS TANKS
○ ASSORTED TOOLS	○ FORDING DEPTHS & ANGLES

TRAIL CONDITIONS

OBSERVATIONS

CONCLUSIONS

YES	NO	SHADE ONE	TRAIL REPUTATION	SCORE
○	○	RECOMMEND OVERALL?		
○	○	WELL MANAGED?		
○	○	CHALLENGING?	1 TO 10	1 TO 10

Off Roading Log

DATE	LOCATION
PASS NEEDED	
DAILY MEMBERSHIP PARK PERMIT	LAND OWNER ORGANIZATION NATIONAL PARK

GROUP OR ORGANIZATION

CHECKLIST	
○ TIRE PRESSURES & SPARE(S)	○ ALL FLUIDS
○ BELTS & HOSES	○ BRAKE PADS & SHOES
○ ALL BOLTS & LUG NUTS	○ SHOCKS & MOUNTS
○ WINCH & BATTERIES	○ ALL SPARE GAS TANKS
○ ASSORTED TOOLS	○ FORDING DEPTHS & ANGLES

TRAIL CONDITIONS

OBSERVATIONS

CONCLUSIONS				
YES	NO	SHADE ONE	TRAIL REPUTATION	SCORE
○	○	RECOMMEND OVERALL?		
○	○	WELL MANAGED?		
○	○	CHALLENGING?	1 TO 10	1 TO 10

Off Roading Log

DATE	LOCATION
PASS NEEDED	
DAILY MEMBERSHIP PARK PERMIT	LAND OWNER ORGANIZATION NATIONAL PARK

GROUP OR ORGANIZATION

CHECKLIST

○ TIRE PRESSURES & SPARE(S)	○ ALL FLUIDS
○ BELTS & HOSES	○ BRAKE PADS & SHOES
○ ALL BOLTS & LUG NUTS	○ SHOCKS & MOUNTS
○ WINCH & BATTERIES	○ ALL SPARE GAS TANKS
○ ASSORTED TOOLS	○ FORDING DEPTHS & ANGLES

TRAIL CONDITIONS

OBSERVATIONS

CONCLUSIONS

YES	NO	SHADE ONE	TRAIL REPUTATION	SCORE
○	○	RECOMMEND OVERALL?		
○	○	WELL MANAGED?		
○	○	CHALLENGING?	1 TO 10	1 TO 10

Off Roading Log

DATE	LOCATION

PASS NEEDED	
DAILY MEMBERSHIP PARK PERMIT	LAND OWNER ORGANIZATION NATIONAL PARK

GROUP OR ORGANIZATION

CHECKLIST

o TIRE PRESSURES & SPARE(S)	o ALL FLUIDS
o BELTS & HOSES	o BRAKE PADS & SHOES
o ALL BOLTS & LUG NUTS	o SHOCKS & MOUNTS
o WINCH & BATTERIES	o ALL SPARE GAS TANKS
o ASSORTED TOOLS	o FORDING DEPTHS & ANGLES

TRAIL CONDITIONS

OBSERVATIONS

CONCLUSIONS

YES	NO	SHADE ONE	TRAIL REPUTATION	SCORE
o	o	RECOMMEND OVERALL?		
o	o	WELL MANAGED?		
o	o	CHALLENGING?	1 TO 10	1 TO 10

Off Roading Log

DATE	LOCATION
PASS NEEDED	
DAILY MEMBERSHIP PARK PERMIT	LAND OWNER ORGANIZATION NATIONAL PARK

GROUP OR ORGANIZATION

CHECKLIST

○ TIRE PRESSURES & SPARE(S)	○ ALL FLUIDS
○ BELTS & HOSES	○ BRAKE PADS & SHOES
○ ALL BOLTS & LUG NUTS	○ SHOCKS & MOUNTS
○ WINCH & BATTERIES	○ ALL SPARE GAS TANKS
○ ASSORTED TOOLS	○ FORDING DEPTHS & ANGLES

TRAIL CONDITIONS

OBSERVATIONS

CONCLUSIONS

YES	NO	SHADE ONE	TRAIL REPUTATION	SCORE
○	○	RECOMMEND OVERALL?		
○	○	WELL MANAGED?		
○	○	CHALLENGING?	1 TO 10	1 TO 10

Off Roading Log

DATE	LOCATION
PASS NEEDED	
DAILY MEMBERSHIP PARK PERMIT	LAND OWNER ORGANIZATION NATIONAL PARK

GROUP OR ORGANIZATION

CHECKLIST	
○ TIRE PRESSURES & SPARE(S)	○ ALL FLUIDS
○ BELTS & HOSES	○ BRAKE PADS & SHOES
○ ALL BOLTS & LUG NUTS	○ SHOCKS & MOUNTS
○ WINCH & BATTERIES	○ ALL SPARE GAS TANKS
○ ASSORTED TOOLS	○ FORDING DEPTHS & ANGLES

TRAIL CONDITIONS

OBSERVATIONS

CONCLUSIONS				
YES	NO	SHADE ONE	TRAIL REPUTATION	SCORE
○	○	RECOMMEND OVERALL?		
○	○	WELL MANAGED?		
○	○	CHALLENGING?	1 TO 10	1 TO 10

Off Roading Log

DATE	LOCATION
PASS NEEDED	
DAILY MEMBERSHIP PARK PERMIT	LAND OWNER ORGANIZATION NATIONAL PARK

GROUP OR ORGANIZATION

CHECKLIST

○ TIRE PRESSURES & SPARE(S)	○ ALL FLUIDS
○ BELTS & HOSES	○ BRAKE PADS & SHOES
○ ALL BOLTS & LUG NUTS	○ SHOCKS & MOUNTS
○ WINCH & BATTERIES	○ ALL SPARE GAS TANKS
○ ASSORTED TOOLS	○ FORDING DEPTHS & ANGLES

TRAIL CONDITIONS

OBSERVATIONS

CONCLUSIONS

YES	NO	SHADE ONE	TRAIL REPUTATION	SCORE
○	○	RECOMMEND OVERALL?		
○	○	WELL MANAGED?		
○	○	CHALLENGING?	1 TO 10	1 TO 10

Off Roading Log

DATE	LOCATION
PASS NEEDED	
DAILY MEMBERSHIP PARK PERMIT	LAND OWNER ORGANIZATION NATIONAL PARK

GROUP OR ORGANIZATION

CHECKLIST	
o TIRE PRESSURES & SPARE(S)	o ALL FLUIDS
o BELTS & HOSES	o BRAKE PADS & SHOES
o ALL BOLTS & LUG NUTS	o SHOCKS & MOUNTS
o WINCH & BATTERIES	o ALL SPARE GAS TANKS
o ASSORTED TOOLS	o FORDING DEPTHS & ANGLES

TRAIL CONDITIONS

OBSERVATIONS

CONCLUSIONS				
YES	NO	SHADE ONE	TRAIL REPUTATION	SCORE
o	o	RECOMMEND OVERALL?		
o	o	WELL MANAGED?		
o	o	CHALLENGING?	1 TO 10	1 TO 10

Off Roading Log

DATE	LOCATION
PASS NEEDED	
DAILY MEMBERSHIP PARK PERMIT	LAND OWNER ORGANIZATION NATIONAL PARK

GROUP OR ORGANIZATION

CHECKLIST

o TIRE PRESSURES & SPARE(S)	o ALL FLUIDS
o BELTS & HOSES	o BRAKE PADS & SHOES
o ALL BOLTS & LUG NUTS	o SHOCKS & MOUNTS
o WINCH & BATTERIES	o ALL SPARE GAS TANKS
o ASSORTED TOOLS	o FORDING DEPTHS & ANGLES

TRAIL CONDITIONS

OBSERVATIONS

CONCLUSIONS

YES	NO	SHADE ONE	TRAIL REPUTATION	SCORE
o	o	RECOMMEND OVERALL?		
o	o	WELL MANAGED?		
o	o	CHALLENGING?	1 TO 10	1 TO 10

Off Roading Log

DATE	LOCATION
PASS NEEDED	
DAILY MEMBERSHIP PARK PERMIT	LAND OWNER ORGANIZATION NATIONAL PARK

GROUP OR ORGANIZATION

CHECKLIST

○ TIRE PRESSURES & SPARE(S)	○ ALL FLUIDS
○ BELTS & HOSES	○ BRAKE PADS & SHOES
○ ALL BOLTS & LUG NUTS	○ SHOCKS & MOUNTS
○ WINCH & BATTERIES	○ ALL SPARE GAS TANKS
○ ASSORTED TOOLS	○ FORDING DEPTHS & ANGLES

TRAIL CONDITIONS

OBSERVATIONS

CONCLUSIONS

YES	NO	SHADE ONE	TRAIL REPUTATION	SCORE
○	○	RECOMMEND OVERALL?		
○	○	WELL MANAGED?		
○	○	CHALLENGING?	1 TO 10	1 TO 10

Off Roading Log

DATE	LOCATION
PASS NEEDED	
DAILY MEMBERSHIP PARK PERMIT	LAND OWNER ORGANIZATION NATIONAL PARK

GROUP OR ORGANIZATION

CHECKLIST

○ TIRE PRESSURES & SPARE(S)	○ ALL FLUIDS
○ BELTS & HOSES	○ BRAKE PADS & SHOES
○ ALL BOLTS & LUG NUTS	○ SHOCKS & MOUNTS
○ WINCH & BATTERIES	○ ALL SPARE GAS TANKS
○ ASSORTED TOOLS	○ FORDING DEPTHS & ANGLES

TRAIL CONDITIONS

OBSERVATIONS

CONCLUSIONS

YES	NO	SHADE ONE	TRAIL REPUTATION	SCORE
○	○	RECOMMEND OVERALL?		
○	○	WELL MANAGED?		
○	○	CHALLENGING?	1 TO 10	1 TO 10

Off Roading Log

DATE	LOCATION
PASS NEEDED	
DAILY MEMBERSHIP PARK PERMIT	LAND OWNER ORGANIZATION NATIONAL PARK

GROUP OR ORGANIZATION

CHECKLIST

○ TIRE PRESSURES & SPARE(S)	○ ALL FLUIDS
○ BELTS & HOSES	○ BRAKE PADS & SHOES
○ ALL BOLTS & LUG NUTS	○ SHOCKS & MOUNTS
○ WINCH & BATTERIES	○ ALL SPARE GAS TANKS
○ ASSORTED TOOLS	○ FORDING DEPTHS & ANGLES

TRAIL CONDITIONS

OBSERVATIONS

CONCLUSIONS

YES	NO	SHADE ONE	TRAIL REPUTATION	SCORE
○	○	RECOMMEND OVERALL?		
○	○	WELL MANAGED?		
○	○	CHALLENGING?	1 TO 10	1 TO 10

Off Roading Log

DATE	LOCATION
PASS NEEDED	
DAILY MEMBERSHIP PARK PERMIT	LAND OWNER ORGANIZATION NATIONAL PARK

GROUP OR ORGANIZATION

CHECKLIST

o TIRE PRESSURES & SPARE(S)	o ALL FLUIDS
o BELTS & HOSES	o BRAKE PADS & SHOES
o ALL BOLTS & LUG NUTS	o SHOCKS & MOUNTS
o WINCH & BATTERIES	o ALL SPARE GAS TANKS
o ASSORTED TOOLS	o FORDING DEPTHS & ANGLES

TRAIL CONDITIONS

OBSERVATIONS

CONCLUSIONS

YES	NO	SHADE ONE	TRAIL REPUTATION	SCORE
o	o	RECOMMEND OVERALL?		
o	o	WELL MANAGED?		
o	o	CHALLENGING?	1 TO 10	1 TO 10

Off Roading Log

DATE	LOCATION
PASS NEEDED	
DAILY MEMBERSHIP PARK PERMIT	LAND OWNER ORGANIZATION NATIONAL PARK

GROUP OR ORGANIZATION

CHECKLIST	
○ TIRE PRESSURES & SPARE(S)	○ ALL FLUIDS
○ BELTS & HOSES	○ BRAKE PADS & SHOES
○ ALL BOLTS & LUG NUTS	○ SHOCKS & MOUNTS
○ WINCH & BATTERIES	○ ALL SPARE GAS TANKS
○ ASSORTED TOOLS	○ FORDING DEPTHS & ANGLES

TRAIL CONDITIONS

OBSERVATIONS

CONCLUSIONS				
YES	NO	SHADE ONE	TRAIL REPUTATION	SCORE
○	○	RECOMMEND OVERALL?		
○	○	WELL MANAGED?		
○	○	CHALLENGING?	1 TO 10	1 TO 10

Off Roading Log

DATE	LOCATION
PASS NEEDED	
DAILY MEMBERSHIP PARK PERMIT	LAND OWNER ORGANIZATION NATIONAL PARK

GROUP OR ORGANIZATION	

CHECKLIST	
o TIRE PRESSURES & SPARE(S)	o ALL FLUIDS
o BELTS & HOSES	o BRAKE PADS & SHOES
o ALL BOLTS & LUG NUTS	o SHOCKS & MOUNTS
o WINCH & BATTERIES	o ALL SPARE GAS TANKS
o ASSORTED TOOLS	o FORDING DEPTHS & ANGLES

TRAIL CONDITIONS

OBSERVATIONS

CONCLUSIONS			
YES	NO	SHADE ONE	TRAIL REPUTATION	SCORE
o	o	RECOMMEND OVERALL?		
o	o	WELL MANAGED?		
o	o	CHALLENGING?	1 TO 10	1 TO 10

Off Roading Log

DATE	LOCATION
PASS NEEDED	
DAILY MEMBERSHIP PARK PERMIT	LAND OWNER ORGANIZATION NATIONAL PARK

GROUP OR ORGANIZATION

CHECKLIST

o TIRE PRESSURES & SPARE(S)	o ALL FLUIDS
o BELTS & HOSES	o BRAKE PADS & SHOES
o ALL BOLTS & LUG NUTS	o SHOCKS & MOUNTS
o WINCH & BATTERIES	o ALL SPARE GAS TANKS
o ASSORTED TOOLS	o FORDING DEPTHS & ANGLES

TRAIL CONDITIONS

OBSERVATIONS

CONCLUSIONS

YES	NO	SHADE ONE	TRAIL REPUTATION	SCORE
○	○	RECOMMEND OVERALL?		
○	○	WELL MANAGED?		
○	○	CHALLENGING?	1 TO 10	1 TO 10

Off Roading Log

DATE	LOCATION
PASS NEEDED	
DAILY MEMBERSHIP PARK PERMIT	LAND OWNER ORGANIZATION NATIONAL PARK

GROUP OR ORGANIZATION

CHECKLIST

○ TIRE PRESSURES & SPARE(S)	○ ALL FLUIDS
○ BELTS & HOSES	○ BRAKE PADS & SHOES
○ ALL BOLTS & LUG NUTS	○ SHOCKS & MOUNTS
○ WINCH & BATTERIES	○ ALL SPARE GAS TANKS
○ ASSORTED TOOLS	○ FORDING DEPTHS & ANGLES

TRAIL CONDITIONS

OBSERVATIONS

CONCLUSIONS

YES	NO	SHADE ONE	TRAIL REPUTATION	SCORE
○	○	RECOMMEND OVERALL?		
○	○	WELL MANAGED?		
○	○	CHALLENGING?	1 TO 10	1 TO 10

Off Roading Log

DATE	LOCATION
PASS NEEDED	
DAILY MEMBERSHIP PARK PERMIT	LAND OWNER ORGANIZATION NATIONAL PARK

GROUP OR ORGANIZATION	

CHECKLIST	
○ TIRE PRESSURES & SPARE(S)	○ ALL FLUIDS
○ BELTS & HOSES	○ BRAKE PADS & SHOES
○ ALL BOLTS & LUG NUTS	○ SHOCKS & MOUNTS
○ WINCH & BATTERIES	○ ALL SPARE GAS TANKS
○ ASSORTED TOOLS	○ FORDING DEPTHS & ANGLES

TRAIL CONDITIONS	

OBSERVATIONS	

CONCLUSIONS				
YES	NO	SHADE ONE	TRAIL REPUTATION	SCORE
○	○	RECOMMEND OVERALL?		
○	○	WELL MANAGED?		
○	○	CHALLENGING?	1 TO 10	1 TO 10

Off Roading Log

DATE	LOCATION
PASS NEEDED	
DAILY MEMBERSHIP PARK PERMIT	LAND OWNER ORGANIZATION NATIONAL PARK

GROUP OR ORGANIZATION

CHECKLIST

o TIRE PRESSURES & SPARE(S)	o ALL FLUIDS
o BELTS & HOSES	o BRAKE PADS & SHOES
o ALL BOLTS & LUG NUTS	o SHOCKS & MOUNTS
o WINCH & BATTERIES	o ALL SPARE GAS TANKS
o ASSORTED TOOLS	o FORDING DEPTHS & ANGLES

TRAIL CONDITIONS

OBSERVATIONS

CONCLUSIONS

YES	NO	SHADE ONE	TRAIL REPUTATION	SCORE
o	o	RECOMMEND OVERALL?		
o	o	WELL MANAGED?		
o	o	CHALLENGING?	1 TO 10	1 TO 10

Off Roading Log

DATE	LOCATION
PASS NEEDED	
DAILY MEMBERSHIP PARK PERMIT	LAND OWNER ORGANIZATION NATIONAL PARK

GROUP OR ORGANIZATION

CHECKLIST	
○ TIRE PRESSURES & SPARE(S)	○ ALL FLUIDS
○ BELTS & HOSES	○ BRAKE PADS & SHOES
○ ALL BOLTS & LUG NUTS	○ SHOCKS & MOUNTS
○ WINCH & BATTERIES	○ ALL SPARE GAS TANKS
○ ASSORTED TOOLS	○ FORDING DEPTHS & ANGLES

TRAIL CONDITIONS

OBSERVATIONS

CONCLUSIONS				
YES	NO	SHADE ONE	TRAIL REPUTATION	SCORE
○	○	RECOMMEND OVERALL?		
○	○	WELL MANAGED?		
○	○	CHALLENGING?	1 TO 10	1 TO 10

Off Roading Log

DATE	LOCATION
PASS NEEDED	
DAILY MEMBERSHIP PARK PERMIT	LAND OWNER ORGANIZATION NATIONAL PARK

GROUP OR ORGANIZATION

CHECKLIST

○ TIRE PRESSURES & SPARE(S)	○ ALL FLUIDS
○ BELTS & HOSES	○ BRAKE PADS & SHOES
○ ALL BOLTS & LUG NUTS	○ SHOCKS & MOUNTS
○ WINCH & BATTERIES	○ ALL SPARE GAS TANKS
○ ASSORTED TOOLS	○ FORDING DEPTHS & ANGLES

TRAIL CONDITIONS

OBSERVATIONS

CONCLUSIONS

YES	NO	SHADE ONE	TRAIL REPUTATION	SCORE
○	○	RECOMMEND OVERALL?		
○	○	WELL MANAGED?		
○	○	CHALLENGING?	1 TO 10	1 TO 10

Off Roading Log

DATE	LOCATION
PASS NEEDED	
DAILY MEMBERSHIP PARK PERMIT	LAND OWNER ORGANIZATION NATIONAL PARK

GROUP OR ORGANIZATION

CHECKLIST

○ TIRE PRESSURES & SPARE(S)	○ ALL FLUIDS
○ BELTS & HOSES	○ BRAKE PADS & SHOES
○ ALL BOLTS & LUG NUTS	○ SHOCKS & MOUNTS
○ WINCH & BATTERIES	○ ALL SPARE GAS TANKS
○ ASSORTED TOOLS	○ FORDING DEPTHS & ANGLES

TRAIL CONDITIONS

OBSERVATIONS

CONCLUSIONS

YES	NO	SHADE ONE	TRAIL REPUTATION	SCORE
○	○	RECOMMEND OVERALL?		
○	○	WELL MANAGED?		
○	○	CHALLENGING?	1 TO 10	1 TO 10

Off Roading Log

DATE	LOCATION
PASS NEEDED	
DAILY MEMBERSHIP PARK PERMIT	LAND OWNER ORGANIZATION NATIONAL PARK

GROUP OR ORGANIZATION

CHECKLIST

○ TIRE PRESSURES & SPARE(S)	○ ALL FLUIDS
○ BELTS & HOSES	○ BRAKE PADS & SHOES
○ ALL BOLTS & LUG NUTS	○ SHOCKS & MOUNTS
○ WINCH & BATTERIES	○ ALL SPARE GAS TANKS
○ ASSORTED TOOLS	○ FORDING DEPTHS & ANGLES

TRAIL CONDITIONS

OBSERVATIONS

CONCLUSIONS

YES	NO	SHADE ONE	TRAIL REPUTATION	SCORE
○	○	RECOMMEND OVERALL?		
○	○	WELL MANAGED?		
○	○	CHALLENGING?	1 TO 10	1 TO 10

Off Roading Log

DATE	LOCATION
PASS NEEDED	
DAILY MEMBERSHIP PARK PERMIT	LAND OWNER ORGANIZATION NATIONAL PARK

GROUP OR ORGANIZATION

CHECKLIST

o TIRE PRESSURES & SPARE(S)	o ALL FLUIDS
o BELTS & HOSES	o BRAKE PADS & SHOES
o ALL BOLTS & LUG NUTS	o SHOCKS & MOUNTS
o WINCH & BATTERIES	o ALL SPARE GAS TANKS
o ASSORTED TOOLS	o FORDING DEPTHS & ANGLES

TRAIL CONDITIONS

OBSERVATIONS

CONCLUSIONS

YES	NO	SHADE ONE	TRAIL REPUTATION	SCORE
o	o	RECOMMEND OVERALL?		
o	o	WELL MANAGED?		
o	o	CHALLENGING?	1 TO 10	1 TO 10

Off Roading Log

DATE	LOCATION
PASS NEEDED	
DAILY MEMBERSHIP PARK PERMIT	LAND OWNER ORGANIZATION NATIONAL PARK

GROUP OR ORGANIZATION

CHECKLIST

○ TIRE PRESSURES & SPARE(S)	○ ALL FLUIDS
○ BELTS & HOSES	○ BRAKE PADS & SHOES
○ ALL BOLTS & LUG NUTS	○ SHOCKS & MOUNTS
○ WINCH & BATTERIES	○ ALL SPARE GAS TANKS
○ ASSORTED TOOLS	○ FORDING DEPTHS & ANGLES

TRAIL CONDITIONS

OBSERVATIONS

CONCLUSIONS

YES	NO	SHADE ONE	TRAIL REPUTATION	SCORE
○	○	RECOMMEND OVERALL?		
○	○	WELL MANAGED?		
○	○	CHALLENGING?	1 TO 10	1 TO 10

Off Roading Log

DATE	LOCATION
PASS NEEDED	
DAILY MEMBERSHIP PARK PERMIT	LAND OWNER ORGANIZATION NATIONAL PARK

GROUP OR ORGANIZATION

CHECKLIST

o TIRE PRESSURES & SPARE(S)	o ALL FLUIDS
o BELTS & HOSES	o BRAKE PADS & SHOES
o ALL BOLTS & LUG NUTS	o SHOCKS & MOUNTS
o WINCH & BATTERIES	o ALL SPARE GAS TANKS
o ASSORTED TOOLS	o FORDING DEPTHS & ANGLES

TRAIL CONDITIONS

OBSERVATIONS

CONCLUSIONS

YES	NO	SHADE ONE	TRAIL REPUTATION	SCORE
o	o	RECOMMEND OVERALL?		
o	o	WELL MANAGED?		
o	o	CHALLENGING?	1 TO 10	1 TO 10

Off Roading Log

DATE	LOCATION
PASS NEEDED	
DAILY MEMBERSHIP PARK PERMIT	LAND OWNER ORGANIZATION NATIONAL PARK

GROUP OR ORGANIZATION

CHECKLIST

o TIRE PRESSURES & SPARE(S)	o ALL FLUIDS
o BELTS & HOSES	o BRAKE PADS & SHOES
o ALL BOLTS & LUG NUTS	o SHOCKS & MOUNTS
o WINCH & BATTERIES	o ALL SPARE GAS TANKS
o ASSORTED TOOLS	o FORDING DEPTHS & ANGLES

TRAIL CONDITIONS

OBSERVATIONS

CONCLUSIONS

YES	NO	SHADE ONE	TRAIL REPUTATION	SCORE
o	o	RECOMMEND OVERALL?		
o	o	WELL MANAGED?		
o	o	CHALLENGING?	1 TO 10	1 TO 10

Off Roading Log

DATE	LOCATION
PASS NEEDED	
DAILY MEMBERSHIP PARK PERMIT	LAND OWNER ORGANIZATION NATIONAL PARK

GROUP OR ORGANIZATION

CHECKLIST

○ TIRE PRESSURES & SPARE(S)	○ ALL FLUIDS
○ BELTS & HOSES	○ BRAKE PADS & SHOES
○ ALL BOLTS & LUG NUTS	○ SHOCKS & MOUNTS
○ WINCH & BATTERIES	○ ALL SPARE GAS TANKS
○ ASSORTED TOOLS	○ FORDING DEPTHS & ANGLES

TRAIL CONDITIONS

OBSERVATIONS

CONCLUSIONS

YES	NO	SHADE ONE	TRAIL REPUTATION	SCORE
○	○	RECOMMEND OVERALL?		
○	○	WELL MANAGED?		
○	○	CHALLENGING?	1 TO 10	1 TO 10

Off Roading Log

DATE	LOCATION
PASS NEEDED	
DAILY MEMBERSHIP PARK PERMIT	LAND OWNER ORGANIZATION NATIONAL PARK

GROUP OR ORGANIZATION	

CHECKLIST	
○ TIRE PRESSURES & SPARE(S)	○ ALL FLUIDS
○ BELTS & HOSES	○ BRAKE PADS & SHOES
○ ALL BOLTS & LUG NUTS	○ SHOCKS & MOUNTS
○ WINCH & BATTERIES	○ ALL SPARE GAS TANKS
○ ASSORTED TOOLS	○ FORDING DEPTHS & ANGLES

TRAIL CONDITIONS	

OBSERVATIONS	

CONCLUSIONS				
YES	NO	SHADE ONE	TRAIL REPUTATION	SCORE
○	○	RECOMMEND OVERALL?		
○	○	WELL MANAGED?		
○	○	CHALLENGING?	1 TO 10	1 TO 10

Off Roading Log

DATE	LOCATION
PASS NEEDED	
DAILY MEMBERSHIP PARK PERMIT	LAND OWNER ORGANIZATION NATIONAL PARK

GROUP OR ORGANIZATION

CHECKLIST

○ TIRE PRESSURES & SPARE(S)	○ ALL FLUIDS
○ BELTS & HOSES	○ BRAKE PADS & SHOES
○ ALL BOLTS & LUG NUTS	○ SHOCKS & MOUNTS
○ WINCH & BATTERIES	○ ALL SPARE GAS TANKS
○ ASSORTED TOOLS	○ FORDING DEPTHS & ANGLES

TRAIL CONDITIONS

OBSERVATIONS

CONCLUSIONS

YES	NO	SHADE ONE	TRAIL REPUTATION	SCORE
○	○	RECOMMEND OVERALL?		
○	○	WELL MANAGED?		
○	○	CHALLENGING?	1 TO 10	1 TO 10

Off Roading Log

DATE	LOCATION
PASS NEEDED	
DAILY MEMBERSHIP PARK PERMIT	LAND OWNER ORGANIZATION NATIONAL PARK

GROUP OR ORGANIZATION

CHECKLIST

o TIRE PRESSURES & SPARE(S)	o ALL FLUIDS
o BELTS & HOSES	o BRAKE PADS & SHOES
o ALL BOLTS & LUG NUTS	o SHOCKS & MOUNTS
o WINCH & BATTERIES	o ALL SPARE GAS TANKS
o ASSORTED TOOLS	o FORDING DEPTHS & ANGLES

TRAIL CONDITIONS

OBSERVATIONS

CONCLUSIONS

YES	NO	SHADE ONE	TRAIL REPUTATION	SCORE
o	o	RECOMMEND OVERALL?		
o	o	WELL MANAGED?		
o	o	CHALLENGING?	1 TO 10	1 TO 10

Off Roading Log

DATE	LOCATION
PASS NEEDED	
DAILY MEMBERSHIP PARK PERMIT	LAND OWNER ORGANIZATION NATIONAL PARK

GROUP OR ORGANIZATION

CHECKLIST

○ TIRE PRESSURES & SPARE(S)	○ ALL FLUIDS
○ BELTS & HOSES	○ BRAKE PADS & SHOES
○ ALL BOLTS & LUG NUTS	○ SHOCKS & MOUNTS
○ WINCH & BATTERIES	○ ALL SPARE GAS TANKS
○ ASSORTED TOOLS	○ FORDING DEPTHS & ANGLES

TRAIL CONDITIONS

OBSERVATIONS

CONCLUSIONS

YES	NO	SHADE ONE	TRAIL REPUTATION	SCORE
○	○	RECOMMEND OVERALL?		
○	○	WELL MANAGED?		
○	○	CHALLENGING?	1 TO 10	1 TO 10

Off Roading Log

DATE	LOCATION
PASS NEEDED	
DAILY MEMBERSHIP PARK PERMIT	LAND OWNER ORGANIZATION NATIONAL PARK

GROUP OR ORGANIZATION

CHECKLIST

○ TIRE PRESSURES & SPARE(S)	○ ALL FLUIDS
○ BELTS & HOSES	○ BRAKE PADS & SHOES
○ ALL BOLTS & LUG NUTS	○ SHOCKS & MOUNTS
○ WINCH & BATTERIES	○ ALL SPARE GAS TANKS
○ ASSORTED TOOLS	○ FORDING DEPTHS & ANGLES

TRAIL CONDITIONS

OBSERVATIONS

CONCLUSIONS

YES	NO	SHADE ONE	TRAIL REPUTATION	SCORE
○	○	RECOMMEND OVERALL?		
○	○	WELL MANAGED?		
○	○	CHALLENGING?	1 TO 10	1 TO 10

Off Roading Log

DATE	LOCATION

PASS NEEDED	
DAILY MEMBERSHIP PARK PERMIT	LAND OWNER ORGANIZATION NATIONAL PARK

GROUP OR ORGANIZATION

CHECKLIST

o TIRE PRESSURES & SPARE(S)	o ALL FLUIDS
o BELTS & HOSES	o BRAKE PADS & SHOES
o ALL BOLTS & LUG NUTS	o SHOCKS & MOUNTS
o WINCH & BATTERIES	o ALL SPARE GAS TANKS
o ASSORTED TOOLS	o FORDING DEPTHS & ANGLES

TRAIL CONDITIONS

OBSERVATIONS

CONCLUSIONS

YES	NO	SHADE ONE	TRAIL REPUTATION	SCORE
o	o	RECOMMEND OVERALL?		
o	o	WELL MANAGED?		
o	o	CHALLENGING?	1 TO 10	1 TO 10

Off Roading Log

DATE	LOCATION

PASS NEEDED	
DAILY MEMBERSHIP PARK PERMIT	LAND OWNER ORGANIZATION NATIONAL PARK

GROUP OR ORGANIZATION

CHECKLIST

○ TIRE PRESSURES & SPARE(S)	○ ALL FLUIDS
○ BELTS & HOSES	○ BRAKE PADS & SHOES
○ ALL BOLTS & LUG NUTS	○ SHOCKS & MOUNTS
○ WINCH & BATTERIES	○ ALL SPARE GAS TANKS
○ ASSORTED TOOLS	○ FORDING DEPTHS & ANGLES

TRAIL CONDITIONS

OBSERVATIONS

CONCLUSIONS

YES	NO	SHADE ONE	TRAIL REPUTATION	SCORE
○	○	RECOMMEND OVERALL?		
○	○	WELL MANAGED?		
○	○	CHALLENGING?	1 TO 10	1 TO 10

Off Roading Log

DATE	LOCATION
PASS NEEDED	
DAILY MEMBERSHIP PARK PERMIT	LAND OWNER ORGANIZATION NATIONAL PARK

GROUP OR ORGANIZATION

CHECKLIST

○ TIRE PRESSURES & SPARE(S)	○ ALL FLUIDS
○ BELTS & HOSES	○ BRAKE PADS & SHOES
○ ALL BOLTS & LUG NUTS	○ SHOCKS & MOUNTS
○ WINCH & BATTERIES	○ ALL SPARE GAS TANKS
○ ASSORTED TOOLS	○ FORDING DEPTHS & ANGLES

TRAIL CONDITIONS

OBSERVATIONS

CONCLUSIONS

YES	NO	SHADE ONE	TRAIL REPUTATION	SCORE
○	○	RECOMMEND OVERALL?		
○	○	WELL MANAGED?		
○	○	CHALLENGING?	1 TO 10	1 TO 10

Off Roading Log

DATE	LOCATION
PASS NEEDED	
DAILY MEMBERSHIP PARK PERMIT	LAND OWNER ORGANIZATION NATIONAL PARK

GROUP OR ORGANIZATION

CHECKLIST

○ TIRE PRESSURES & SPARE(S)	○ ALL FLUIDS
○ BELTS & HOSES	○ BRAKE PADS & SHOES
○ ALL BOLTS & LUG NUTS	○ SHOCKS & MOUNTS
○ WINCH & BATTERIES	○ ALL SPARE GAS TANKS
○ ASSORTED TOOLS	○ FORDING DEPTHS & ANGLES

TRAIL CONDITIONS

OBSERVATIONS

CONCLUSIONS

YES	NO	SHADE ONE	TRAIL REPUTATION	SCORE
○	○	RECOMMEND OVERALL?		
○	○	WELL MANAGED?		
○	○	CHALLENGING?	1 TO 10	1 TO 10

Off Roading Log

DATE	LOCATION
PASS NEEDED	
DAILY MEMBERSHIP PARK PERMIT	LAND OWNER ORGANIZATION NATIONAL PARK

GROUP OR ORGANIZATION

CHECKLIST

○ TIRE PRESSURES & SPARE(S)	○ ALL FLUIDS
○ BELTS & HOSES	○ BRAKE PADS & SHOES
○ ALL BOLTS & LUG NUTS	○ SHOCKS & MOUNTS
○ WINCH & BATTERIES	○ ALL SPARE GAS TANKS
○ ASSORTED TOOLS	○ FORDING DEPTHS & ANGLES

TRAIL CONDITIONS

OBSERVATIONS

CONCLUSIONS

YES	NO	SHADE ONE	TRAIL REPUTATION	SCORE
○	○	RECOMMEND OVERALL?		
○	○	WELL MANAGED?		
○	○	CHALLENGING?	1 TO 10	1 TO 10

Off Roading Log

DATE	LOCATION
PASS NEEDED	
DAILY MEMBERSHIP PARK PERMIT	LAND OWNER ORGANIZATION NATIONAL PARK

GROUP OR ORGANIZATION

CHECKLIST	
o TIRE PRESSURES & SPARE(S)	o ALL FLUIDS
o BELTS & HOSES	o BRAKE PADS & SHOES
o ALL BOLTS & LUG NUTS	o SHOCKS & MOUNTS
o WINCH & BATTERIES	o ALL SPARE GAS TANKS
o ASSORTED TOOLS	o FORDING DEPTHS & ANGLES

TRAIL CONDITIONS

OBSERVATIONS

CONCLUSIONS				
YES	NO	SHADE ONE	TRAIL REPUTATION	SCORE
o	o	RECOMMEND OVERALL?		
o	o	WELL MANAGED?		
o	o	CHALLENGING?	1 TO 10	1 TO 10

Off Roading Log

DATE	LOCATION
PASS NEEDED	
DAILY MEMBERSHIP PARK PERMIT	LAND OWNER ORGANIZATION NATIONAL PARK

GROUP OR ORGANIZATION

CHECKLIST

o TIRE PRESSURES & SPARE(S)	o ALL FLUIDS
o BELTS & HOSES	o BRAKE PADS & SHOES
o ALL BOLTS & LUG NUTS	o SHOCKS & MOUNTS
o WINCH & BATTERIES	o ALL SPARE GAS TANKS
o ASSORTED TOOLS	o FORDING DEPTHS & ANGLES

TRAIL CONDITIONS

OBSERVATIONS

CONCLUSIONS

YES	NO	SHADE ONE	TRAIL REPUTATION	SCORE
o	o	RECOMMEND OVERALL?		
o	o	WELL MANAGED?		
o	o	CHALLENGING?	1 TO 10	1 TO 10

Off Roading Log

DATE	LOCATION

PASS NEEDED	
DAILY MEMBERSHIP PARK PERMIT	LAND OWNER ORGANIZATION NATIONAL PARK

GROUP OR ORGANIZATION

CHECKLIST

○ TIRE PRESSURES & SPARE(S)	○ ALL FLUIDS
○ BELTS & HOSES	○ BRAKE PADS & SHOES
○ ALL BOLTS & LUG NUTS	○ SHOCKS & MOUNTS
○ WINCH & BATTERIES	○ ALL SPARE GAS TANKS
○ ASSORTED TOOLS	○ FORDING DEPTHS & ANGLES

TRAIL CONDITIONS

OBSERVATIONS

CONCLUSIONS

YES	NO	SHADE ONE	TRAIL REPUTATION	SCORE
○	○	RECOMMEND OVERALL?		
○	○	WELL MANAGED?		
○	○	CHALLENGING?	1 TO 10	1 TO 10

Off Roading Log

DATE	LOCATION
PASS NEEDED	
DAILY MEMBERSHIP PARK PERMIT	LAND OWNER ORGANIZATION NATIONAL PARK

GROUP OR ORGANIZATION

CHECKLIST

○ TIRE PRESSURES & SPARE(S)	○ ALL FLUIDS
○ BELTS & HOSES	○ BRAKE PADS & SHOES
○ ALL BOLTS & LUG NUTS	○ SHOCKS & MOUNTS
○ WINCH & BATTERIES	○ ALL SPARE GAS TANKS
○ ASSORTED TOOLS	○ FORDING DEPTHS & ANGLES

TRAIL CONDITIONS

OBSERVATIONS

CONCLUSIONS

YES	NO	SHADE ONE	TRAIL REPUTATION	SCORE
○	○	RECOMMEND OVERALL?		
○	○	WELL MANAGED?		
○	○	CHALLENGING?	1 TO 10	1 TO 10

Off Roading Log

DATE	LOCATION
PASS NEEDED	
DAILY MEMBERSHIP PARK PERMIT	LAND OWNER ORGANIZATION NATIONAL PARK

GROUP OR ORGANIZATION

CHECKLIST

○ TIRE PRESSURES & SPARE(S)	○ ALL FLUIDS
○ BELTS & HOSES	○ BRAKE PADS & SHOES
○ ALL BOLTS & LUG NUTS	○ SHOCKS & MOUNTS
○ WINCH & BATTERIES	○ ALL SPARE GAS TANKS
○ ASSORTED TOOLS	○ FORDING DEPTHS & ANGLES

TRAIL CONDITIONS

OBSERVATIONS

CONCLUSIONS

YES	NO	SHADE ONE	TRAIL REPUTATION	SCORE
○	○	RECOMMEND OVERALL?		
○	○	WELL MANAGED?		
○	○	CHALLENGING?	1 TO 10	1 TO 10

Off Roading Log

DATE	LOCATION
PASS NEEDED	
DAILY MEMBERSHIP PARK PERMIT	LAND OWNER ORGANIZATION NATIONAL PARK

GROUP OR ORGANIZATION

CHECKLIST

○ TIRE PRESSURES & SPARE(S)	○ ALL FLUIDS
○ BELTS & HOSES	○ BRAKE PADS & SHOES
○ ALL BOLTS & LUG NUTS	○ SHOCKS & MOUNTS
○ WINCH & BATTERIES	○ ALL SPARE GAS TANKS
○ ASSORTED TOOLS	○ FORDING DEPTHS & ANGLES

TRAIL CONDITIONS

OBSERVATIONS

CONCLUSIONS

YES	NO	SHADE ONE	TRAIL REPUTATION	SCORE
○	○	RECOMMEND OVERALL?		
○	○	WELL MANAGED?		
○	○	CHALLENGING?	1 TO 10	1 TO 10

Off Roading Log

DATE	LOCATION
PASS NEEDED	
DAILY MEMBERSHIP PARK PERMIT	LAND OWNER ORGANIZATION NATIONAL PARK

GROUP OR ORGANIZATION

CHECKLIST

○ TIRE PRESSURES & SPARE(S)	○ ALL FLUIDS
○ BELTS & HOSES	○ BRAKE PADS & SHOES
○ ALL BOLTS & LUG NUTS	○ SHOCKS & MOUNTS
○ WINCH & BATTERIES	○ ALL SPARE GAS TANKS
○ ASSORTED TOOLS	○ FORDING DEPTHS & ANGLES

TRAIL CONDITIONS

OBSERVATIONS

CONCLUSIONS

YES	NO	SHADE ONE	TRAIL REPUTATION	SCORE
○	○	RECOMMEND OVERALL?		
○	○	WELL MANAGED?		
○	○	CHALLENGING?	1 TO 10	1 TO 10

Off Roading Log

DATE	LOCATION

PASS NEEDED	
DAILY MEMBERSHIP PARK PERMIT	LAND OWNER ORGANIZATION NATIONAL PARK

GROUP OR ORGANIZATION

CHECKLIST

o TIRE PRESSURES & SPARE(S)	o ALL FLUIDS
o BELTS & HOSES	o BRAKE PADS & SHOES
o ALL BOLTS & LUG NUTS	o SHOCKS & MOUNTS
o WINCH & BATTERIES	o ALL SPARE GAS TANKS
o ASSORTED TOOLS	o FORDING DEPTHS & ANGLES

TRAIL CONDITIONS

OBSERVATIONS

CONCLUSIONS

YES	NO	SHADE ONE	TRAIL REPUTATION	SCORE
o	o	RECOMMEND OVERALL?		
o	o	WELL MANAGED?		
o	o	CHALLENGING?	1 TO 10	1 TO 10

Off Roading Log

DATE	LOCATION
PASS NEEDED	
DAILY MEMBERSHIP PARK PERMIT	LAND OWNER ORGANIZATION NATIONAL PARK

GROUP OR ORGANIZATION

CHECKLIST

o TIRE PRESSURES & SPARE(S)	o ALL FLUIDS
o BELTS & HOSES	o BRAKE PADS & SHOES
o ALL BOLTS & LUG NUTS	o SHOCKS & MOUNTS
o WINCH & BATTERIES	o ALL SPARE GAS TANKS
o ASSORTED TOOLS	o FORDING DEPTHS & ANGLES

TRAIL CONDITIONS

OBSERVATIONS

CONCLUSIONS

YES	NO	SHADE ONE	TRAIL REPUTATION	SCORE
o	o	RECOMMEND OVERALL?		
o	o	WELL MANAGED?		
o	o	CHALLENGING?	1 TO 10	1 TO 10

Off Roading Log

DATE	LOCATION
PASS NEEDED	
DAILY MEMBERSHIP PARK PERMIT	LAND OWNER ORGANIZATION NATIONAL PARK

GROUP OR ORGANIZATION

CHECKLIST

o TIRE PRESSURES & SPARE(S)	o ALL FLUIDS
o BELTS & HOSES	o BRAKE PADS & SHOES
o ALL BOLTS & LUG NUTS	o SHOCKS & MOUNTS
o WINCH & BATTERIES	o ALL SPARE GAS TANKS
o ASSORTED TOOLS	o FORDING DEPTHS & ANGLES

TRAIL CONDITIONS

OBSERVATIONS

CONCLUSIONS

YES	NO	SHADE ONE	TRAIL REPUTATION	SCORE
o	o	RECOMMEND OVERALL?		
o	o	WELL MANAGED?		
o	o	CHALLENGING?	1 TO 10	1 TO 10

Off Roading Log

DATE	LOCATION
PASS NEEDED	
DAILY MEMBERSHIP PARK PERMIT	LAND OWNER ORGANIZATION NATIONAL PARK

GROUP OR ORGANIZATION

CHECKLIST

○ TIRE PRESSURES & SPARE(S)	○ ALL FLUIDS
○ BELTS & HOSES	○ BRAKE PADS & SHOES
○ ALL BOLTS & LUG NUTS	○ SHOCKS & MOUNTS
○ WINCH & BATTERIES	○ ALL SPARE GAS TANKS
○ ASSORTED TOOLS	○ FORDING DEPTHS & ANGLES

TRAIL CONDITIONS

OBSERVATIONS

CONCLUSIONS

YES	NO	SHADE ONE	TRAIL REPUTATION	SCORE
○	○	RECOMMEND OVERALL?		
○	○	WELL MANAGED?		
○	○	CHALLENGING?	1 TO 10	1 TO 10

Off Roading Log

DATE	LOCATION
PASS NEEDED	
DAILY MEMBERSHIP PARK PERMIT	LAND OWNER ORGANIZATION NATIONAL PARK

GROUP OR ORGANIZATION

CHECKLIST

o TIRE PRESSURES & SPARE(S)	o ALL FLUIDS
o BELTS & HOSES	o BRAKE PADS & SHOES
o ALL BOLTS & LUG NUTS	o SHOCKS & MOUNTS
o WINCH & BATTERIES	o ALL SPARE GAS TANKS
o ASSORTED TOOLS	o FORDING DEPTHS & ANGLES

TRAIL CONDITIONS

OBSERVATIONS

CONCLUSIONS

YES	NO	SHADE ONE	TRAIL REPUTATION	SCORE
o	o	RECOMMEND OVERALL?		
o	o	WELL MANAGED?		
o	o	CHALLENGING?	1 TO 10	1 TO 10

Off Roading Log

DATE	LOCATION
PASS NEEDED	
DAILY MEMBERSHIP PARK PERMIT	LAND OWNER ORGANIZATION NATIONAL PARK

GROUP OR ORGANIZATION

CHECKLIST

o TIRE PRESSURES & SPARE(S)	o ALL FLUIDS
o BELTS & HOSES	o BRAKE PADS & SHOES
o ALL BOLTS & LUG NUTS	o SHOCKS & MOUNTS
o WINCH & BATTERIES	o ALL SPARE GAS TANKS
o ASSORTED TOOLS	o FORDING DEPTHS & ANGLES

TRAIL CONDITIONS

OBSERVATIONS

CONCLUSIONS

YES	NO	SHADE ONE	TRAIL REPUTATION	SCORE
o	o	RECOMMEND OVERALL?		
o	o	WELL MANAGED?		
o	o	CHALLENGING?	1 TO 10	1 TO 10

Off Roading Log

DATE	LOCATION

PASS NEEDED	
DAILY MEMBERSHIP PARK PERMIT	LAND OWNER ORGANIZATION NATIONAL PARK

GROUP OR ORGANIZATION

CHECKLIST	
o TIRE PRESSURES & SPARE(S)	o ALL FLUIDS
o BELTS & HOSES	o BRAKE PADS & SHOES
o ALL BOLTS & LUG NUTS	o SHOCKS & MOUNTS
o WINCH & BATTERIES	o ALL SPARE GAS TANKS
o ASSORTED TOOLS	o FORDING DEPTHS & ANGLES

TRAIL CONDITIONS

OBSERVATIONS

CONCLUSIONS

YES	NO	SHADE ONE	TRAIL REPUTATION	SCORE
o	o	RECOMMEND OVERALL?		
o	o	WELL MANAGED?		
o	o	CHALLENGING?	1 TO 10	1 TO 10

Off Roading Log

DATE	LOCATION
PASS NEEDED	
DAILY MEMBERSHIP PARK PERMIT	LAND OWNER ORGANIZATION NATIONAL PARK

GROUP OR ORGANIZATION

CHECKLIST	
○ TIRE PRESSURES & SPARE(S)	○ ALL FLUIDS
○ BELTS & HOSES	○ BRAKE PADS & SHOES
○ ALL BOLTS & LUG NUTS	○ SHOCKS & MOUNTS
○ WINCH & BATTERIES	○ ALL SPARE GAS TANKS
○ ASSORTED TOOLS	○ FORDING DEPTHS & ANGLES

TRAIL CONDITIONS

OBSERVATIONS

CONCLUSIONS				
YES	NO	SHADE ONE	TRAIL REPUTATION	SCORE
○	○	RECOMMEND OVERALL?		
○	○	WELL MANAGED?		
○	○	CHALLENGING?	1 TO 10	1 TO 10

Off Roading Log

DATE	LOCATION

PASS NEEDED	
DAILY MEMBERSHIP PARK PERMIT	LAND OWNER ORGANIZATION NATIONAL PARK

GROUP OR ORGANIZATION

CHECKLIST

○ TIRE PRESSURES & SPARE(S)	○ ALL FLUIDS
○ BELTS & HOSES	○ BRAKE PADS & SHOES
○ ALL BOLTS & LUG NUTS	○ SHOCKS & MOUNTS
○ WINCH & BATTERIES	○ ALL SPARE GAS TANKS
○ ASSORTED TOOLS	○ FORDING DEPTHS & ANGLES

TRAIL CONDITIONS

OBSERVATIONS

CONCLUSIONS

YES	NO	SHADE ONE	TRAIL REPUTATION	SCORE
○	○	RECOMMEND OVERALL?		
○	○	WELL MANAGED?		
○	○	CHALLENGING?	1 TO 10	1 TO 10

Off Roading Log

DATE	LOCATION
PASS NEEDED	
DAILY MEMBERSHIP PARK PERMIT	LAND OWNER ORGANIZATION NATIONAL PARK

GROUP OR ORGANIZATION

CHECKLIST	
○ TIRE PRESSURES & SPARE(S)	○ ALL FLUIDS
○ BELTS & HOSES	○ BRAKE PADS & SHOES
○ ALL BOLTS & LUG NUTS	○ SHOCKS & MOUNTS
○ WINCH & BATTERIES	○ ALL SPARE GAS TANKS
○ ASSORTED TOOLS	○ FORDING DEPTHS & ANGLES

TRAIL CONDITIONS

OBSERVATIONS

CONCLUSIONS			
YES	NO	SHADE ONE	TRAIL REPUTATION	SCORE
○	○	RECOMMEND OVERALL?		
○	○	WELL MANAGED?		
○	○	CHALLENGING?	1 TO 10	1 TO 10

Off Roading Log

DATE	LOCATION
PASS NEEDED	
DAILY MEMBERSHIP PARK PERMIT	LAND OWNER ORGANIZATION NATIONAL PARK

GROUP OR ORGANIZATION

CHECKLIST

o TIRE PRESSURES & SPARE(S)	o ALL FLUIDS
o BELTS & HOSES	o BRAKE PADS & SHOES
o ALL BOLTS & LUG NUTS	o SHOCKS & MOUNTS
o WINCH & BATTERIES	o ALL SPARE GAS TANKS
o ASSORTED TOOLS	o FORDING DEPTHS & ANGLES

TRAIL CONDITIONS

OBSERVATIONS

CONCLUSIONS

YES	NO	SHADE ONE	TRAIL REPUTATION	SCORE
o	o	RECOMMEND OVERALL?		
o	o	WELL MANAGED?		
o	o	CHALLENGING?	1 TO 10	1 TO 10

Off Roading Log

DATE	LOCATION
PASS NEEDED	
DAILY MEMBERSHIP PARK PERMIT	LAND OWNER ORGANIZATION NATIONAL PARK

GROUP OR ORGANIZATION

CHECKLIST

○ TIRE PRESSURES & SPARE(S)	○ ALL FLUIDS
○ BELTS & HOSES	○ BRAKE PADS & SHOES
○ ALL BOLTS & LUG NUTS	○ SHOCKS & MOUNTS
○ WINCH & BATTERIES	○ ALL SPARE GAS TANKS
○ ASSORTED TOOLS	○ FORDING DEPTHS & ANGLES

TRAIL CONDITIONS

OBSERVATIONS

CONCLUSIONS

YES	NO	SHADE ONE	TRAIL REPUTATION	SCORE
○	○	RECOMMEND OVERALL?		
○	○	WELL MANAGED?		
○	○	CHALLENGING?	1 TO 10	1 TO 10

Off Roading Log

DATE	LOCATION
PASS NEEDED	
DAILY MEMBERSHIP PARK PERMIT	LAND OWNER ORGANIZATION NATIONAL PARK

GROUP OR ORGANIZATION

CHECKLIST

○ TIRE PRESSURES & SPARE(S)	○ ALL FLUIDS
○ BELTS & HOSES	○ BRAKE PADS & SHOES
○ ALL BOLTS & LUG NUTS	○ SHOCKS & MOUNTS
○ WINCH & BATTERIES	○ ALL SPARE GAS TANKS
○ ASSORTED TOOLS	○ FORDING DEPTHS & ANGLES

TRAIL CONDITIONS

OBSERVATIONS

CONCLUSIONS

YES	NO	SHADE ONE	TRAIL REPUTATION	SCORE
○	○	RECOMMEND OVERALL?		
○	○	WELL MANAGED?		
○	○	CHALLENGING?	1 TO 10	1 TO 10

Off Roading Log

DATE	LOCATION
PASS NEEDED	
DAILY MEMBERSHIP PARK PERMIT	LAND OWNER ORGANIZATION NATIONAL PARK

GROUP OR ORGANIZATION

CHECKLIST

○ TIRE PRESSURES & SPARE(S)	○ ALL FLUIDS
○ BELTS & HOSES	○ BRAKE PADS & SHOES
○ ALL BOLTS & LUG NUTS	○ SHOCKS & MOUNTS
○ WINCH & BATTERIES	○ ALL SPARE GAS TANKS
○ ASSORTED TOOLS	○ FORDING DEPTHS & ANGLES

TRAIL CONDITIONS

OBSERVATIONS

CONCLUSIONS

YES	NO	SHADE ONE	TRAIL REPUTATION	SCORE
○	○	RECOMMEND OVERALL?		
○	○	WELL MANAGED?		
○	○	CHALLENGING?	1 TO 10	1 TO 10

Off Roading Log

DATE	LOCATION
PASS NEEDED	
DAILY MEMBERSHIP PARK PERMIT	LAND OWNER ORGANIZATION NATIONAL PARK

GROUP OR ORGANIZATION

CHECKLIST

○ TIRE PRESSURES & SPARE(S)	○ ALL FLUIDS
○ BELTS & HOSES	○ BRAKE PADS & SHOES
○ ALL BOLTS & LUG NUTS	○ SHOCKS & MOUNTS
○ WINCH & BATTERIES	○ ALL SPARE GAS TANKS
○ ASSORTED TOOLS	○ FORDING DEPTHS & ANGLES

TRAIL CONDITIONS

OBSERVATIONS

CONCLUSIONS

YES	NO	SHADE ONE	TRAIL REPUTATION	SCORE
○	○	RECOMMEND OVERALL?		
○	○	WELL MANAGED?		
○	○	CHALLENGING?	1 TO 10	1 TO 10

Off Roading Log

DATE	LOCATION
PASS NEEDED	
DAILY MEMBERSHIP PARK PERMIT	LAND OWNER ORGANIZATION NATIONAL PARK

GROUP OR ORGANIZATION

CHECKLIST

○ TIRE PRESSURES & SPARE(S)	○ ALL FLUIDS
○ BELTS & HOSES	○ BRAKE PADS & SHOES
○ ALL BOLTS & LUG NUTS	○ SHOCKS & MOUNTS
○ WINCH & BATTERIES	○ ALL SPARE GAS TANKS
○ ASSORTED TOOLS	○ FORDING DEPTHS & ANGLES

TRAIL CONDITIONS

OBSERVATIONS

CONCLUSIONS

YES	NO	SHADE ONE	TRAIL REPUTATION	SCORE
○	○	RECOMMEND OVERALL?		
○	○	WELL MANAGED?		
○	○	CHALLENGING?	1 TO 10	1 TO 10

Off Roading Log

DATE	LOCATION
PASS NEEDED	
DAILY MEMBERSHIP PARK PERMIT	LAND OWNER ORGANIZATION NATIONAL PARK

GROUP OR ORGANIZATION

CHECKLIST

○ TIRE PRESSURES & SPARE(S)	○ ALL FLUIDS
○ BELTS & HOSES	○ BRAKE PADS & SHOES
○ ALL BOLTS & LUG NUTS	○ SHOCKS & MOUNTS
○ WINCH & BATTERIES	○ ALL SPARE GAS TANKS
○ ASSORTED TOOLS	○ FORDING DEPTHS & ANGLES

TRAIL CONDITIONS

OBSERVATIONS

CONCLUSIONS

YES	NO	SHADE ONE	TRAIL REPUTATION	SCORE
○	○	RECOMMEND OVERALL?		
○	○	WELL MANAGED?		
○	○	CHALLENGING?	1 TO 10	1 TO 10

Off Roading Log

DATE	LOCATION
PASS NEEDED	
DAILY MEMBERSHIP PARK PERMIT	LAND OWNER ORGANIZATION NATIONAL PARK

GROUP OR ORGANIZATION

CHECKLIST

○ TIRE PRESSURES & SPARE(S)	○ ALL FLUIDS
○ BELTS & HOSES	○ BRAKE PADS & SHOES
○ ALL BOLTS & LUG NUTS	○ SHOCKS & MOUNTS
○ WINCH & BATTERIES	○ ALL SPARE GAS TANKS
○ ASSORTED TOOLS	○ FORDING DEPTHS & ANGLES

TRAIL CONDITIONS

OBSERVATIONS

CONCLUSIONS

YES	NO	SHADE ONE	TRAIL REPUTATION	SCORE
○	○	RECOMMEND OVERALL?		
○	○	WELL MANAGED?		
○	○	CHALLENGING?	1 TO 10	1 TO 10

Off Roading Log

DATE	LOCATION
PASS NEEDED	
DAILY MEMBERSHIP PARK PERMIT	LAND OWNER ORGANIZATION NATIONAL PARK

GROUP OR ORGANIZATION

CHECKLIST

○ TIRE PRESSURES & SPARE(S)	○ ALL FLUIDS
○ BELTS & HOSES	○ BRAKE PADS & SHOES
○ ALL BOLTS & LUG NUTS	○ SHOCKS & MOUNTS
○ WINCH & BATTERIES	○ ALL SPARE GAS TANKS
○ ASSORTED TOOLS	○ FORDING DEPTHS & ANGLES

TRAIL CONDITIONS

OBSERVATIONS

CONCLUSIONS

YES	NO	SHADE ONE	TRAIL REPUTATION	SCORE
○	○	RECOMMEND OVERALL?		
○	○	WELL MANAGED?		
○	○	CHALLENGING?	1 TO 10	1 TO 10

Off Roading Log

DATE	LOCATION
PASS NEEDED	
DAILY MEMBERSHIP PARK PERMIT	LAND OWNER ORGANIZATION NATIONAL PARK

GROUP OR ORGANIZATION

CHECKLIST

○ TIRE PRESSURES & SPARE(S)	○ ALL FLUIDS
○ BELTS & HOSES	○ BRAKE PADS & SHOES
○ ALL BOLTS & LUG NUTS	○ SHOCKS & MOUNTS
○ WINCH & BATTERIES	○ ALL SPARE GAS TANKS
○ ASSORTED TOOLS	○ FORDING DEPTHS & ANGLES

TRAIL CONDITIONS

OBSERVATIONS

CONCLUSIONS

YES	NO	SHADE ONE	TRAIL REPUTATION	SCORE
○	○	RECOMMEND OVERALL?		
○	○	WELL MANAGED?		
○	○	CHALLENGING?	1 TO 10	1 TO 10

Off Roading Log

DATE	LOCATION
PASS NEEDED	
DAILY MEMBERSHIP PARK PERMIT	LAND OWNER ORGANIZATION NATIONAL PARK

GROUP OR ORGANIZATION

CHECKLIST

○ TIRE PRESSURES & SPARE(S)	○ ALL FLUIDS
○ BELTS & HOSES	○ BRAKE PADS & SHOES
○ ALL BOLTS & LUG NUTS	○ SHOCKS & MOUNTS
○ WINCH & BATTERIES	○ ALL SPARE GAS TANKS
○ ASSORTED TOOLS	○ FORDING DEPTHS & ANGLES

TRAIL CONDITIONS

OBSERVATIONS

CONCLUSIONS

YES	NO	SHADE ONE	TRAIL REPUTATION	SCORE
○	○	RECOMMEND OVERALL?		
○	○	WELL MANAGED?		
○	○	CHALLENGING?	1 TO 10	1 TO 10

Off Roading Log

DATE	LOCATION
PASS NEEDED	
DAILY MEMBERSHIP PARK PERMIT	LAND OWNER ORGANIZATION NATIONAL PARK

GROUP OR ORGANIZATION

CHECKLIST

o TIRE PRESSURES & SPARE(S)	o ALL FLUIDS
o BELTS & HOSES	o BRAKE PADS & SHOES
o ALL BOLTS & LUG NUTS	o SHOCKS & MOUNTS
o WINCH & BATTERIES	o ALL SPARE GAS TANKS
o ASSORTED TOOLS	o FORDING DEPTHS & ANGLES

TRAIL CONDITIONS

OBSERVATIONS

CONCLUSIONS

YES	NO	SHADE ONE	TRAIL REPUTATION	SCORE
o	o	RECOMMEND OVERALL?		
o	o	WELL MANAGED?		
o	o	CHALLENGING?	1 TO 10	1 TO 10

Off Roading Log

DATE	LOCATION
PASS NEEDED	
DAILY MEMBERSHIP PARK PERMIT	LAND OWNER ORGANIZATION NATIONAL PARK

GROUP OR ORGANIZATION

CHECKLIST

o TIRE PRESSURES & SPARE(S)	o ALL FLUIDS
o BELTS & HOSES	o BRAKE PADS & SHOES
o ALL BOLTS & LUG NUTS	o SHOCKS & MOUNTS
o WINCH & BATTERIES	o ALL SPARE GAS TANKS
o ASSORTED TOOLS	o FORDING DEPTHS & ANGLES

TRAIL CONDITIONS

OBSERVATIONS

CONCLUSIONS

YES	NO	SHADE ONE	TRAIL REPUTATION	SCORE
o	o	RECOMMEND OVERALL?		
o	o	WELL MANAGED?		
o	o	CHALLENGING?	1 TO 10	1 TO 10

Off Roading Log

DATE	LOCATION
PASS NEEDED	
DAILY MEMBERSHIP PARK PERMIT	LAND OWNER ORGANIZATION NATIONAL PARK

GROUP OR ORGANIZATION

CHECKLIST

o TIRE PRESSURES & SPARE(S)	o ALL FLUIDS
o BELTS & HOSES	o BRAKE PADS & SHOES
o ALL BOLTS & LUG NUTS	o SHOCKS & MOUNTS
o WINCH & BATTERIES	o ALL SPARE GAS TANKS
o ASSORTED TOOLS	o FORDING DEPTHS & ANGLES

TRAIL CONDITIONS

OBSERVATIONS

CONCLUSIONS

YES	NO	SHADE ONE	TRAIL REPUTATION	SCORE
o	o	RECOMMEND OVERALL?		
o	o	WELL MANAGED?		
o	o	CHALLENGING?	1 TO 10	1 TO 10

Off Roading Log

DATE	LOCATION

PASS NEEDED	
DAILY MEMBERSHIP PARK PERMIT	LAND OWNER ORGANIZATION NATIONAL PARK

GROUP OR ORGANIZATION

CHECKLIST	
○ TIRE PRESSURES & SPARE(S)	○ ALL FLUIDS
○ BELTS & HOSES	○ BRAKE PADS & SHOES
○ ALL BOLTS & LUG NUTS	○ SHOCKS & MOUNTS
○ WINCH & BATTERIES	○ ALL SPARE GAS TANKS
○ ASSORTED TOOLS	○ FORDING DEPTHS & ANGLES

TRAIL CONDITIONS

OBSERVATIONS

CONCLUSIONS				
YES	NO	SHADE ONE	TRAIL REPUTATION	SCORE
○	○	RECOMMEND OVERALL?		
○	○	WELL MANAGED?		
○	○	CHALLENGING?	1 TO 10	1 TO 10

Off Roading Log

DATE	LOCATION
PASS NEEDED	
DAILY MEMBERSHIP PARK PERMIT	LAND OWNER ORGANIZATION NATIONAL PARK

GROUP OR ORGANIZATION

CHECKLIST

○ TIRE PRESSURES & SPARE(S)	○ ALL FLUIDS
○ BELTS & HOSES	○ BRAKE PADS & SHOES
○ ALL BOLTS & LUG NUTS	○ SHOCKS & MOUNTS
○ WINCH & BATTERIES	○ ALL SPARE GAS TANKS
○ ASSORTED TOOLS	○ FORDING DEPTHS & ANGLES

TRAIL CONDITIONS

OBSERVATIONS

CONCLUSIONS

YES	NO	SHADE ONE	TRAIL REPUTATION	SCORE
○	○	RECOMMEND OVERALL?		
○	○	WELL MANAGED?		
○	○	CHALLENGING?	1 TO 10	1 TO 10

Off Roading Log

DATE	LOCATION
PASS NEEDED	
DAILY MEMBERSHIP PARK PERMIT	LAND OWNER ORGANIZATION NATIONAL PARK

GROUP OR ORGANIZATION

CHECKLIST

○ TIRE PRESSURES & SPARE(S)	○ ALL FLUIDS
○ BELTS & HOSES	○ BRAKE PADS & SHOES
○ ALL BOLTS & LUG NUTS	○ SHOCKS & MOUNTS
○ WINCH & BATTERIES	○ ALL SPARE GAS TANKS
○ ASSORTED TOOLS	○ FORDING DEPTHS & ANGLES

TRAIL CONDITIONS

OBSERVATIONS

CONCLUSIONS

YES	NO	SHADE ONE	TRAIL REPUTATION	SCORE
○	○	RECOMMEND OVERALL?		
○	○	WELL MANAGED?		
○	○	CHALLENGING?	1 TO 10	1 TO 10

Off Roading Log

DATE	LOCATION
PASS NEEDED	
DAILY MEMBERSHIP PARK PERMIT	LAND OWNER ORGANIZATION NATIONAL PARK

GROUP OR ORGANIZATION

CHECKLIST

○ TIRE PRESSURES & SPARE(S)	○ ALL FLUIDS
○ BELTS & HOSES	○ BRAKE PADS & SHOES
○ ALL BOLTS & LUG NUTS	○ SHOCKS & MOUNTS
○ WINCH & BATTERIES	○ ALL SPARE GAS TANKS
○ ASSORTED TOOLS	○ FORDING DEPTHS & ANGLES

TRAIL CONDITIONS

OBSERVATIONS

CONCLUSIONS

YES	NO	SHADE ONE	TRAIL REPUTATION	SCORE
○	○	RECOMMEND OVERALL?		
○	○	WELL MANAGED?		
○	○	CHALLENGING?	1 TO 10	1 TO 10

Off Roading Log

DATE	LOCATION
PASS NEEDED	
DAILY MEMBERSHIP PARK PERMIT	LAND OWNER ORGANIZATION NATIONAL PARK

GROUP OR ORGANIZATION

CHECKLIST

○ TIRE PRESSURES & SPARE(S)	○ ALL FLUIDS
○ BELTS & HOSES	○ BRAKE PADS & SHOES
○ ALL BOLTS & LUG NUTS	○ SHOCKS & MOUNTS
○ WINCH & BATTERIES	○ ALL SPARE GAS TANKS
○ ASSORTED TOOLS	○ FORDING DEPTHS & ANGLES

TRAIL CONDITIONS

OBSERVATIONS

CONCLUSIONS

YES	NO	SHADE ONE	TRAIL REPUTATION	SCORE
○	○	RECOMMEND OVERALL?		
○	○	WELL MANAGED?		
○	○	CHALLENGING?	1 TO 10	1 TO 10

Off Roading Log

DATE	LOCATION
PASS NEEDED	
DAILY MEMBERSHIP PARK PERMIT	LAND OWNER ORGANIZATION NATIONAL PARK

GROUP OR ORGANIZATION

CHECKLIST

○ TIRE PRESSURES & SPARE(S)	○ ALL FLUIDS
○ BELTS & HOSES	○ BRAKE PADS & SHOES
○ ALL BOLTS & LUG NUTS	○ SHOCKS & MOUNTS
○ WINCH & BATTERIES	○ ALL SPARE GAS TANKS
○ ASSORTED TOOLS	○ FORDING DEPTHS & ANGLES

TRAIL CONDITIONS

OBSERVATIONS

CONCLUSIONS

YES	NO	SHADE ONE	TRAIL REPUTATION	SCORE
○	○	RECOMMEND OVERALL?		
○	○	WELL MANAGED?		
○	○	CHALLENGING?	1 TO 10	1 TO 10

Off Roading Log

DATE	LOCATION
PASS NEEDED	
DAILY MEMBERSHIP PARK PERMIT	LAND OWNER ORGANIZATION NATIONAL PARK

GROUP OR ORGANIZATION	

CHECKLIST	
o TIRE PRESSURES & SPARE(S)	o ALL FLUIDS
o BELTS & HOSES	o BRAKE PADS & SHOES
o ALL BOLTS & LUG NUTS	o SHOCKS & MOUNTS
o WINCH & BATTERIES	o ALL SPARE GAS TANKS
o ASSORTED TOOLS	o FORDING DEPTHS & ANGLES

TRAIL CONDITIONS

OBSERVATIONS

CONCLUSIONS				
YES	NO	SHADE ONE	TRAIL REPUTATION	SCORE
o	o	RECOMMEND OVERALL?		
o	o	WELL MANAGED?		
o	o	CHALLENGING?	1 TO 10	1 TO 10

Off Roading Log

DATE	LOCATION
PASS NEEDED	
DAILY MEMBERSHIP PARK PERMIT	LAND OWNER ORGANIZATION NATIONAL PARK

GROUP OR ORGANIZATION

CHECKLIST

○ TIRE PRESSURES & SPARE(S)	○ ALL FLUIDS
○ BELTS & HOSES	○ BRAKE PADS & SHOES
○ ALL BOLTS & LUG NUTS	○ SHOCKS & MOUNTS
○ WINCH & BATTERIES	○ ALL SPARE GAS TANKS
○ ASSORTED TOOLS	○ FORDING DEPTHS & ANGLES

TRAIL CONDITIONS

OBSERVATIONS

CONCLUSIONS

YES	NO	SHADE ONE	TRAIL REPUTATION	SCORE
○	○	RECOMMEND OVERALL?		
○	○	WELL MANAGED?		
○	○	CHALLENGING?	1 TO 10	1 TO 10

Off Roading Log

DATE	LOCATION
PASS NEEDED	
DAILY MEMBERSHIP PARK PERMIT	LAND OWNER ORGANIZATION NATIONAL PARK

GROUP OR ORGANIZATION

CHECKLIST	
o TIRE PRESSURES & SPARE(S)	o ALL FLUIDS
o BELTS & HOSES	o BRAKE PADS & SHOES
o ALL BOLTS & LUG NUTS	o SHOCKS & MOUNTS
o WINCH & BATTERIES	o ALL SPARE GAS TANKS
o ASSORTED TOOLS	o FORDING DEPTHS & ANGLES

TRAIL CONDITIONS

OBSERVATIONS

CONCLUSIONS				
YES	NO	SHADE ONE	TRAIL REPUTATION	SCORE
o	o	RECOMMEND OVERALL?		
o	o	WELL MANAGED?		
o	o	CHALLENGING?	1 TO 10	1 TO 10

Off Roading Log

DATE	LOCATION
PASS NEEDED	
DAILY MEMBERSHIP PARK PERMIT	LAND OWNER ORGANIZATION NATIONAL PARK

GROUP OR ORGANIZATION

CHECKLIST

○ TIRE PRESSURES & SPARE(S)	○ ALL FLUIDS
○ BELTS & HOSES	○ BRAKE PADS & SHOES
○ ALL BOLTS & LUG NUTS	○ SHOCKS & MOUNTS
○ WINCH & BATTERIES	○ ALL SPARE GAS TANKS
○ ASSORTED TOOLS	○ FORDING DEPTHS & ANGLES

TRAIL CONDITIONS

OBSERVATIONS

CONCLUSIONS

YES	NO	SHADE ONE	TRAIL REPUTATION	SCORE
○	○	RECOMMEND OVERALL?		
○	○	WELL MANAGED?		
○	○	CHALLENGING?	1 TO 10	1 TO 10

Off Roading Log

DATE	LOCATION
PASS NEEDED	
DAILY MEMBERSHIP PARK PERMIT	LAND OWNER ORGANIZATION NATIONAL PARK

GROUP OR ORGANIZATION

CHECKLIST

○ TIRE PRESSURES & SPARE(S)	○ ALL FLUIDS
○ BELTS & HOSES	○ BRAKE PADS & SHOES
○ ALL BOLTS & LUG NUTS	○ SHOCKS & MOUNTS
○ WINCH & BATTERIES	○ ALL SPARE GAS TANKS
○ ASSORTED TOOLS	○ FORDING DEPTHS & ANGLES

TRAIL CONDITIONS

OBSERVATIONS

CONCLUSIONS

YES	NO	SHADE ONE	TRAIL REPUTATION	SCORE
○	○	RECOMMEND OVERALL?		
○	○	WELL MANAGED?		
○	○	CHALLENGING?	1 TO 10	1 TO 10

www.ingramcontent.com/pod-product-compliance
Lightning Source LLC
Chambersburg PA
CBHW071407080526
44587CB00017B/3207